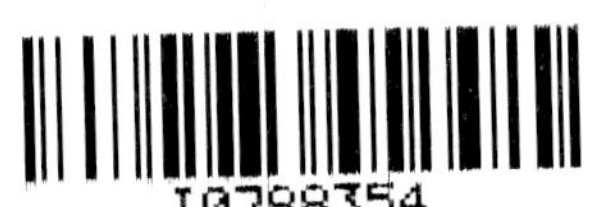

This Book belong To:

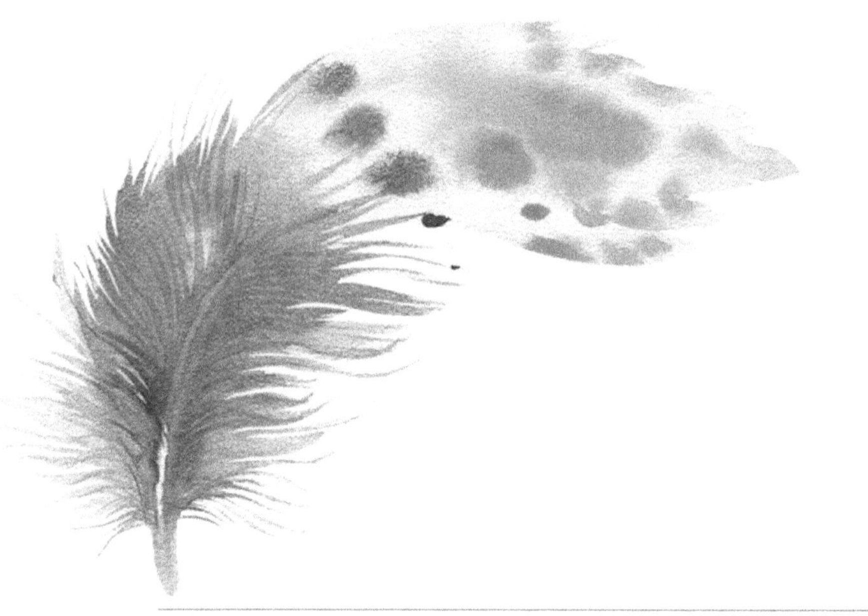

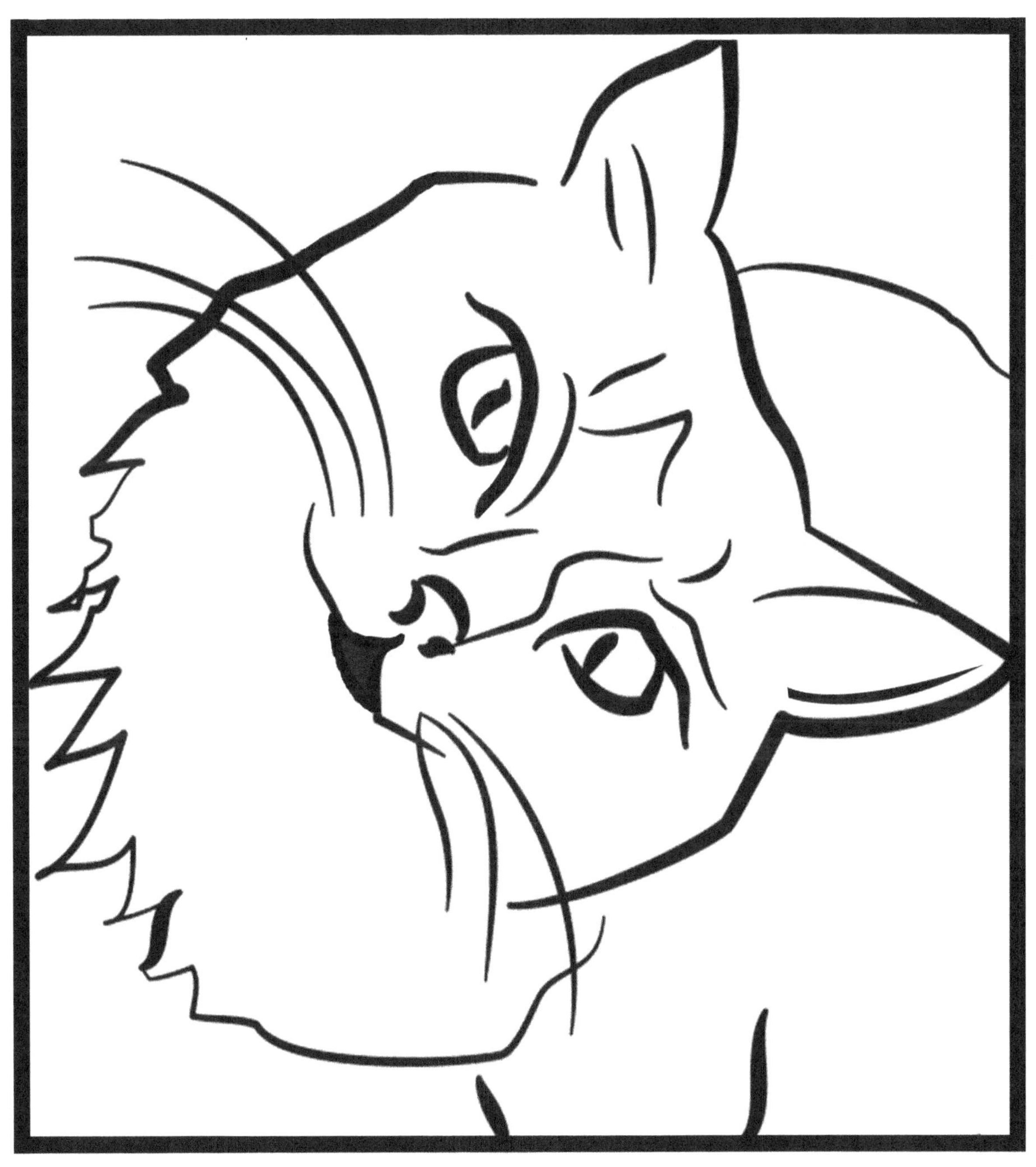

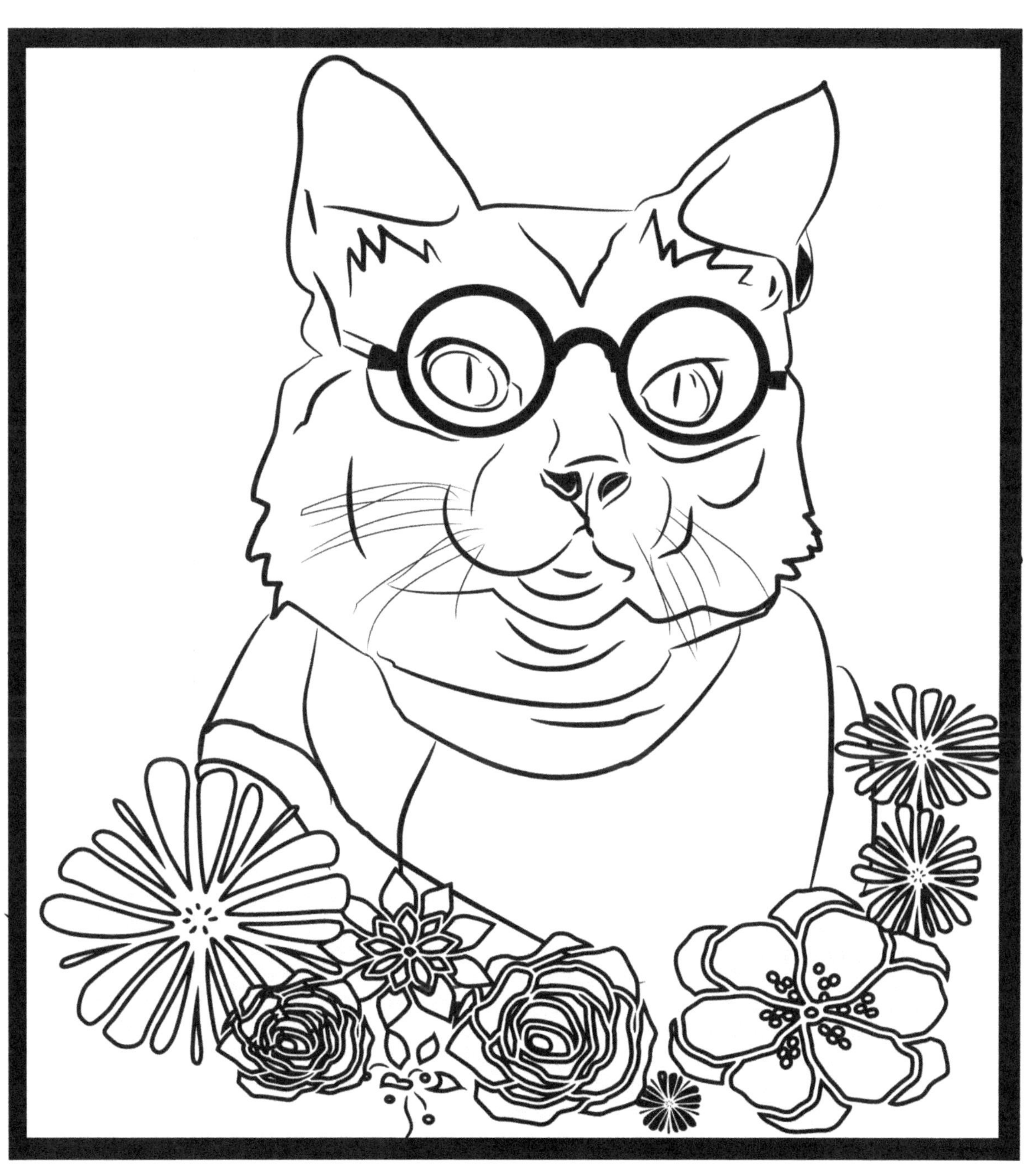

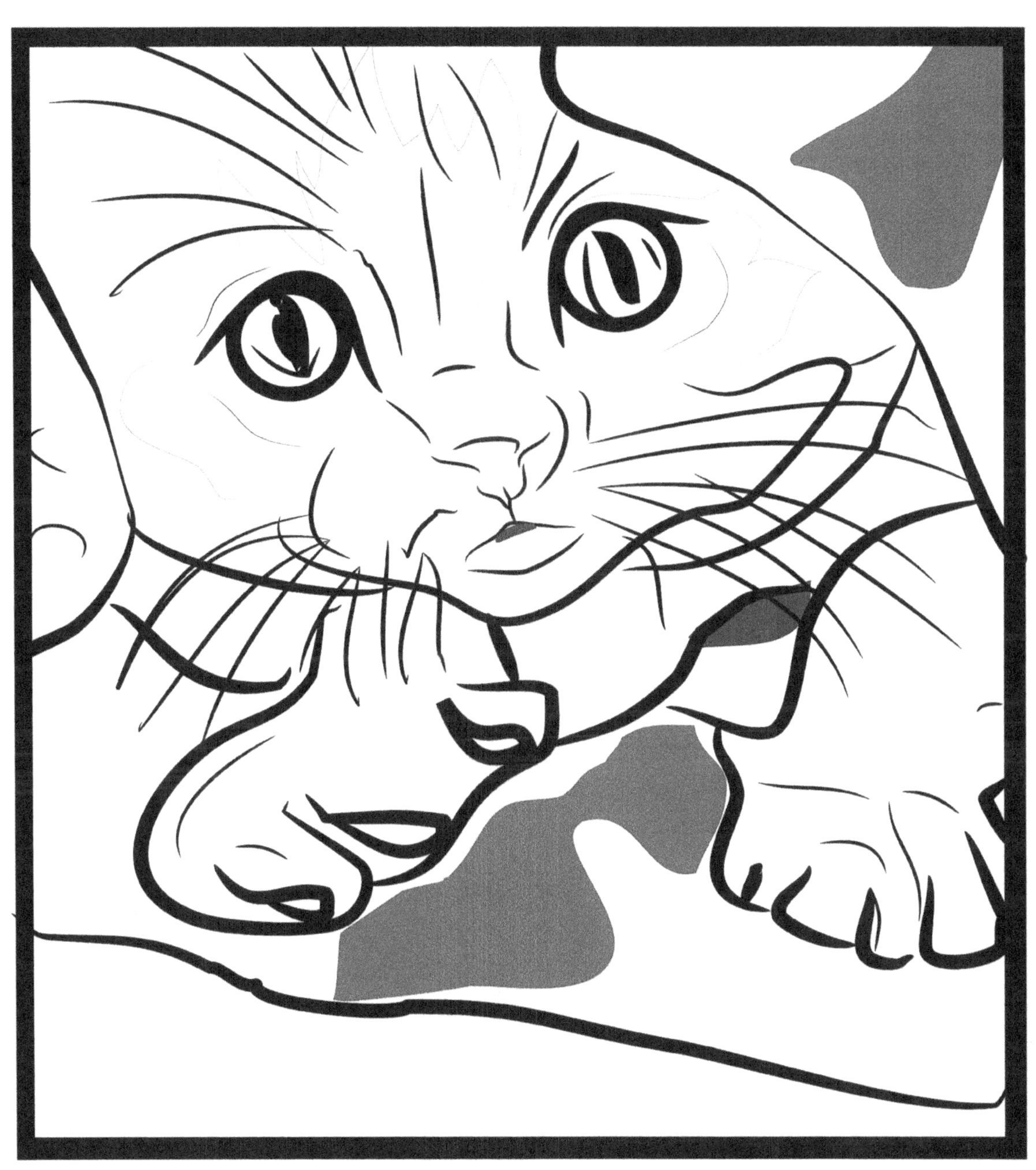

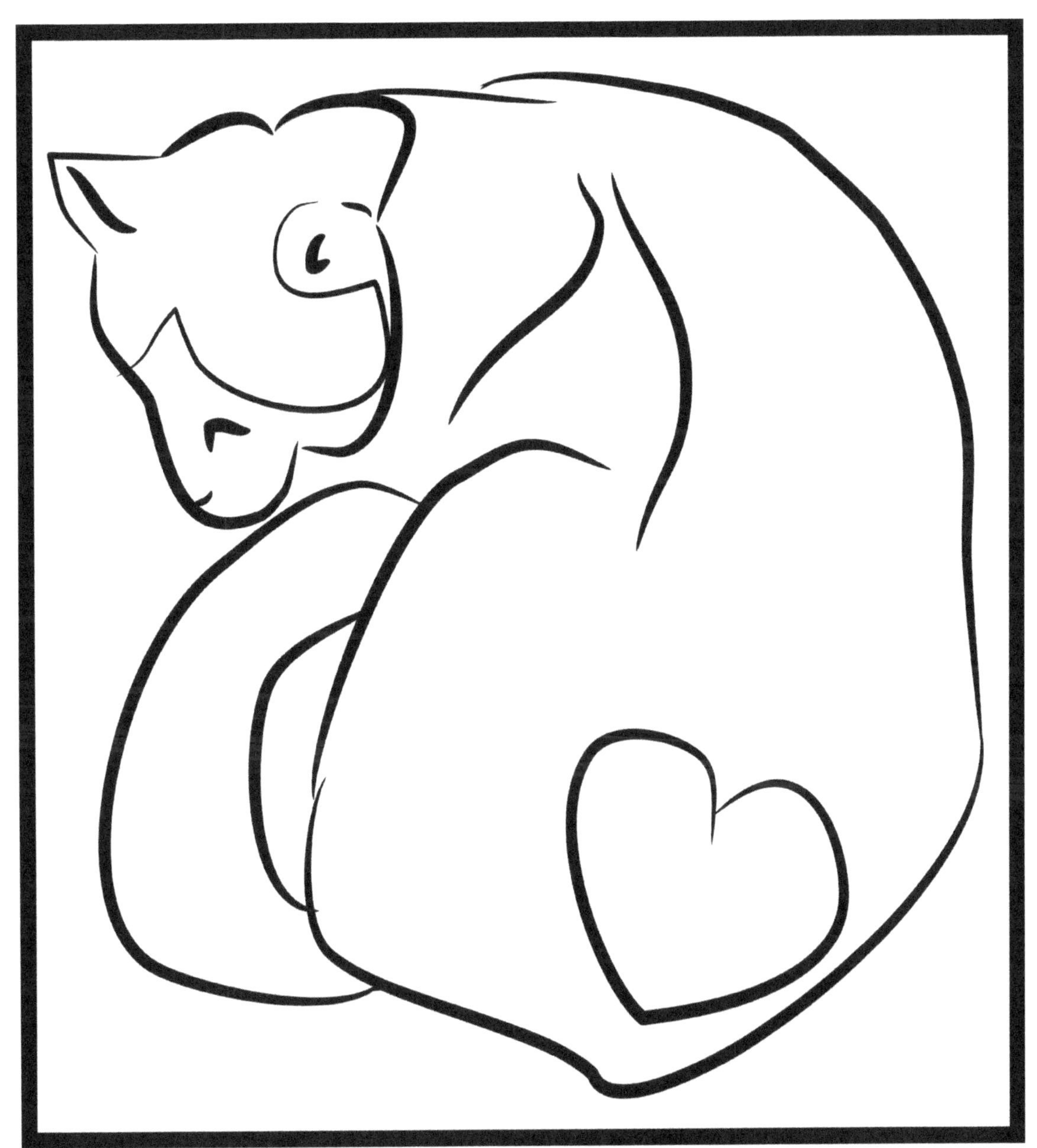

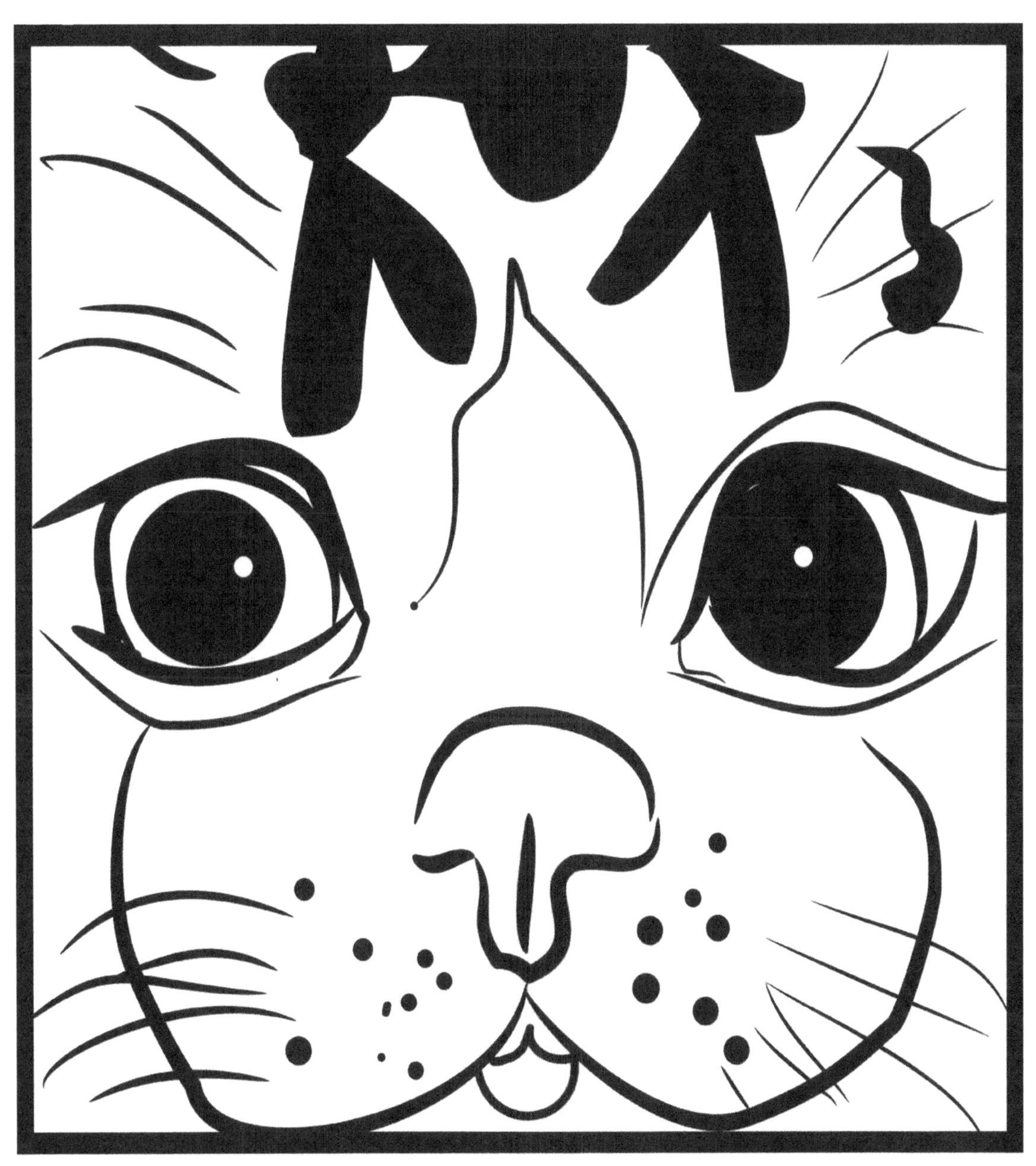

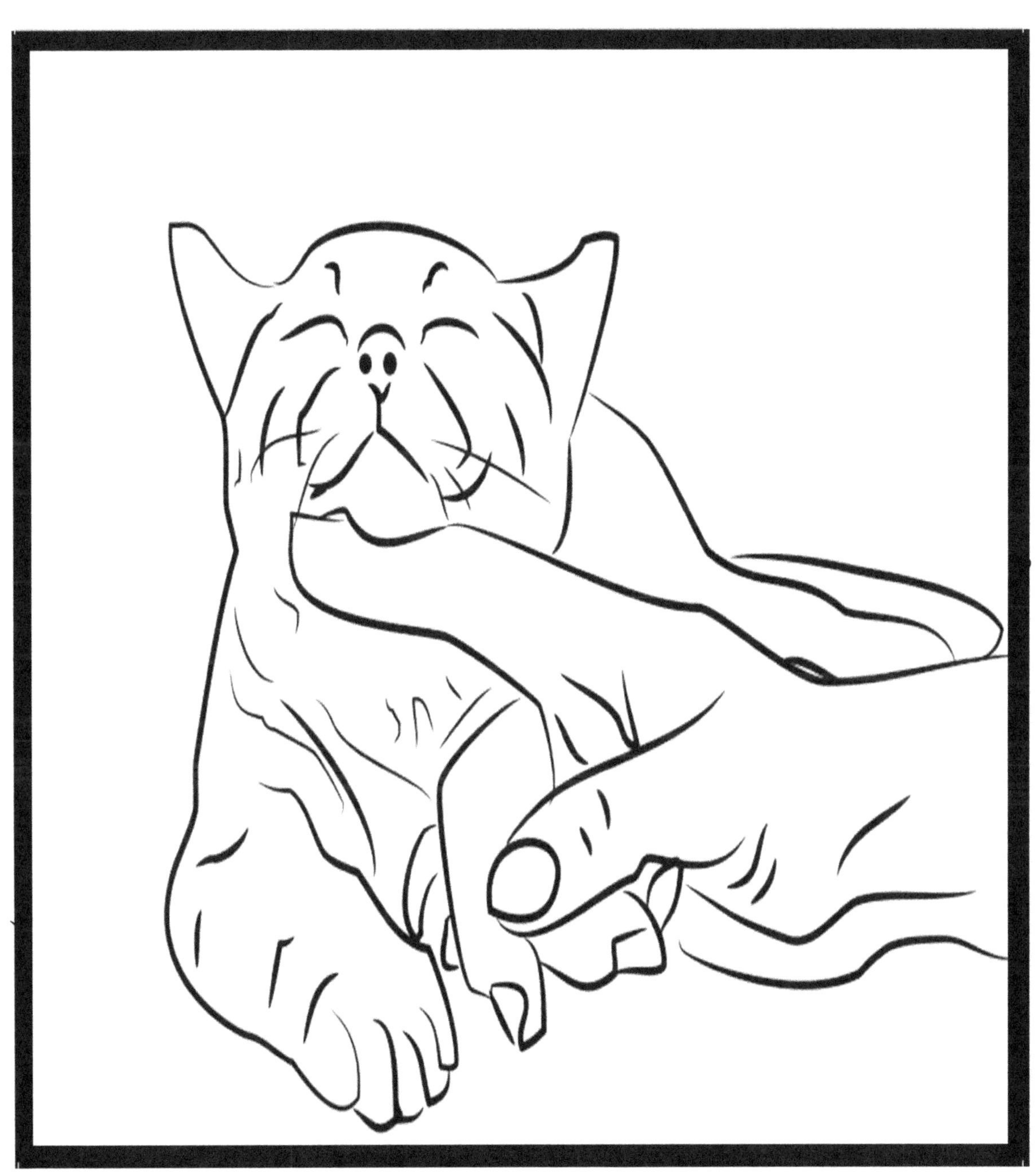

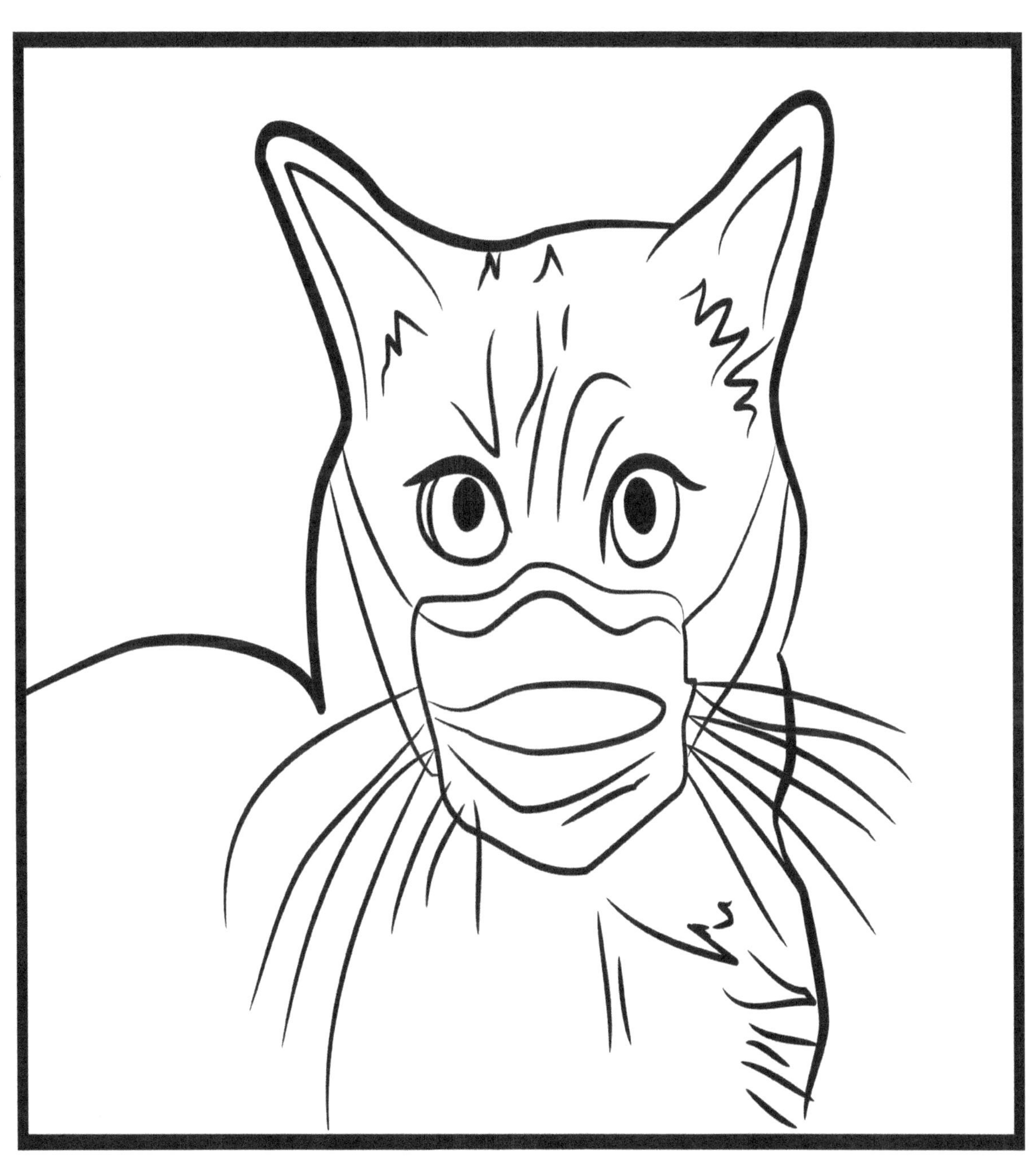

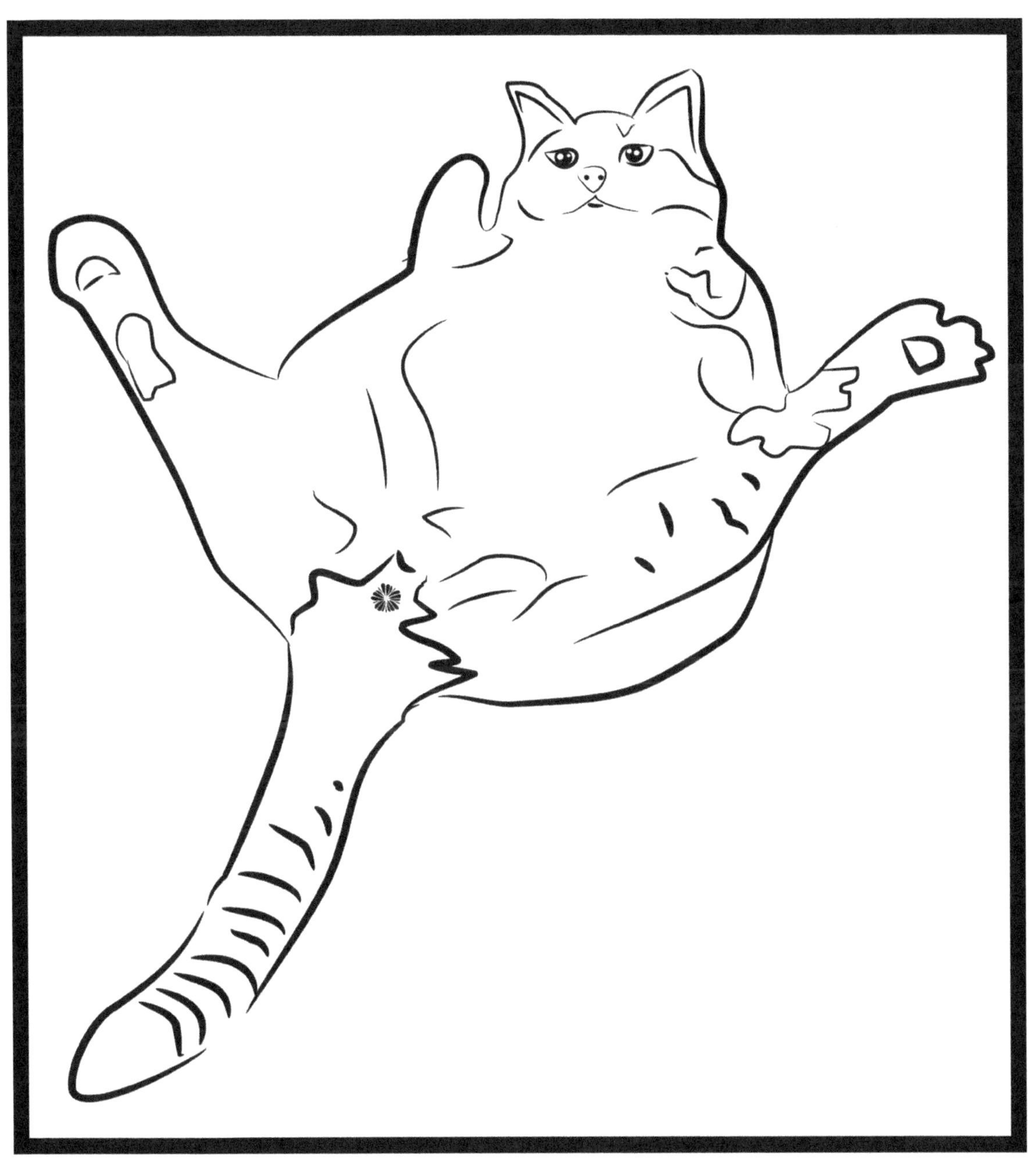

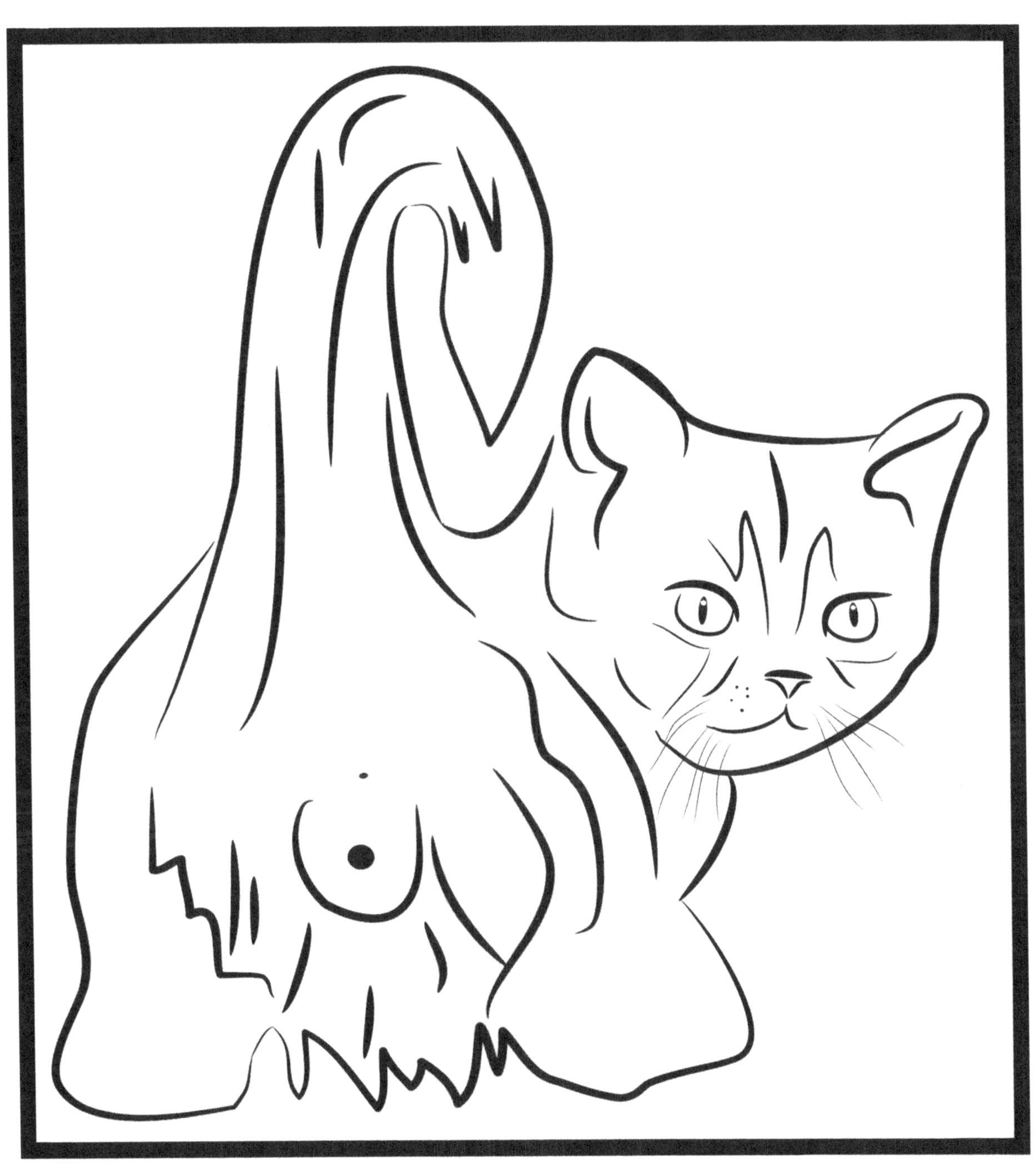

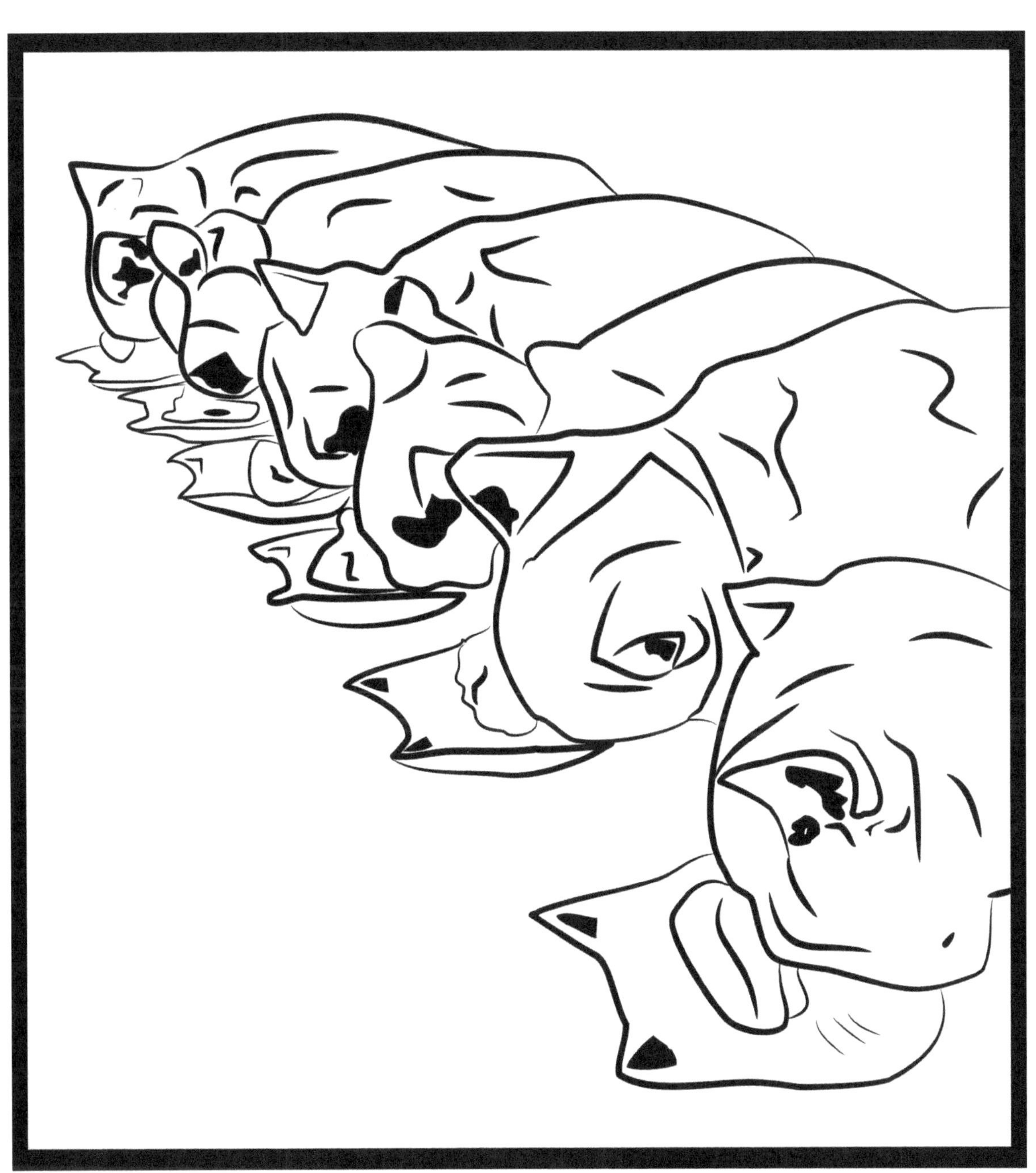

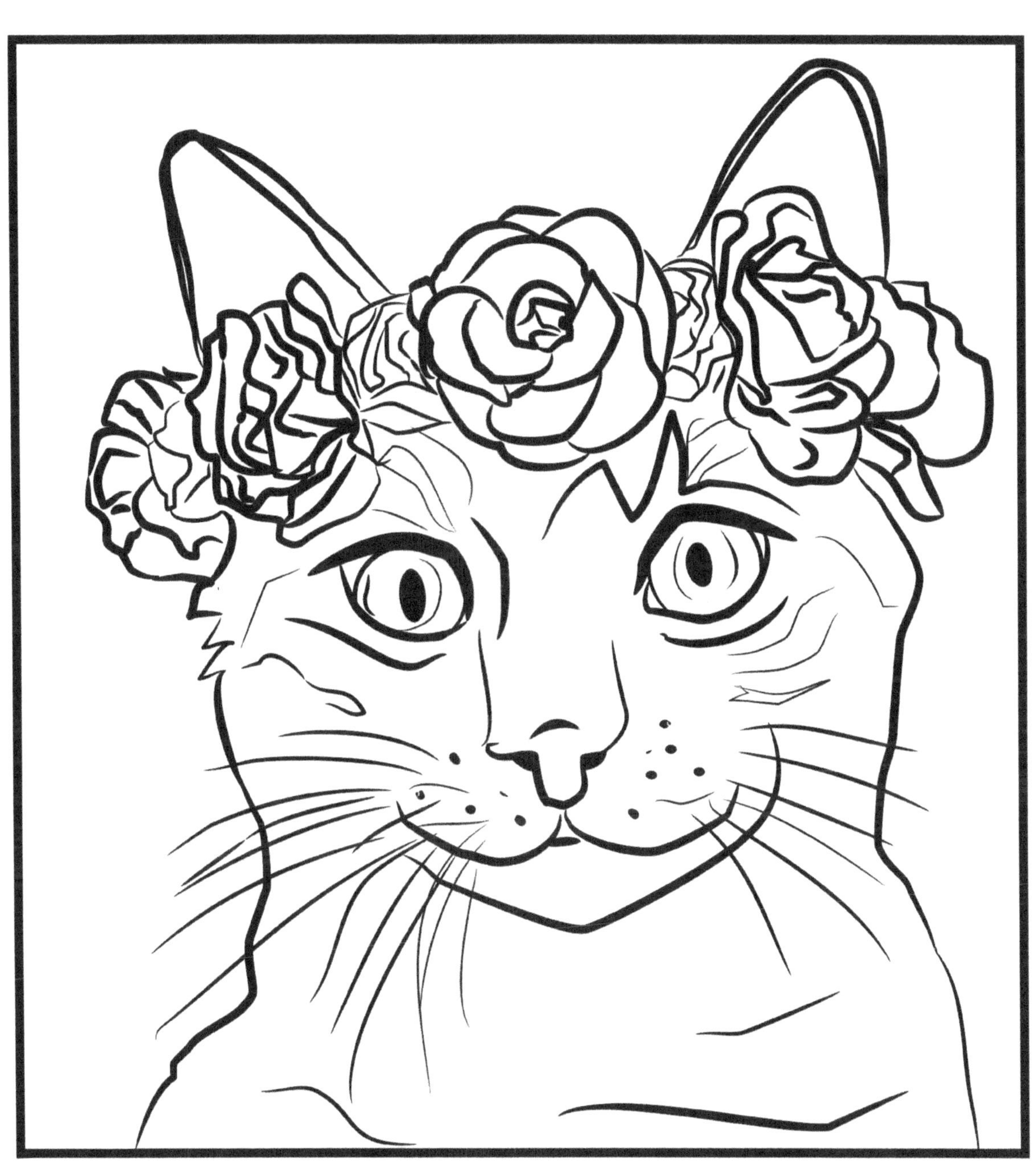

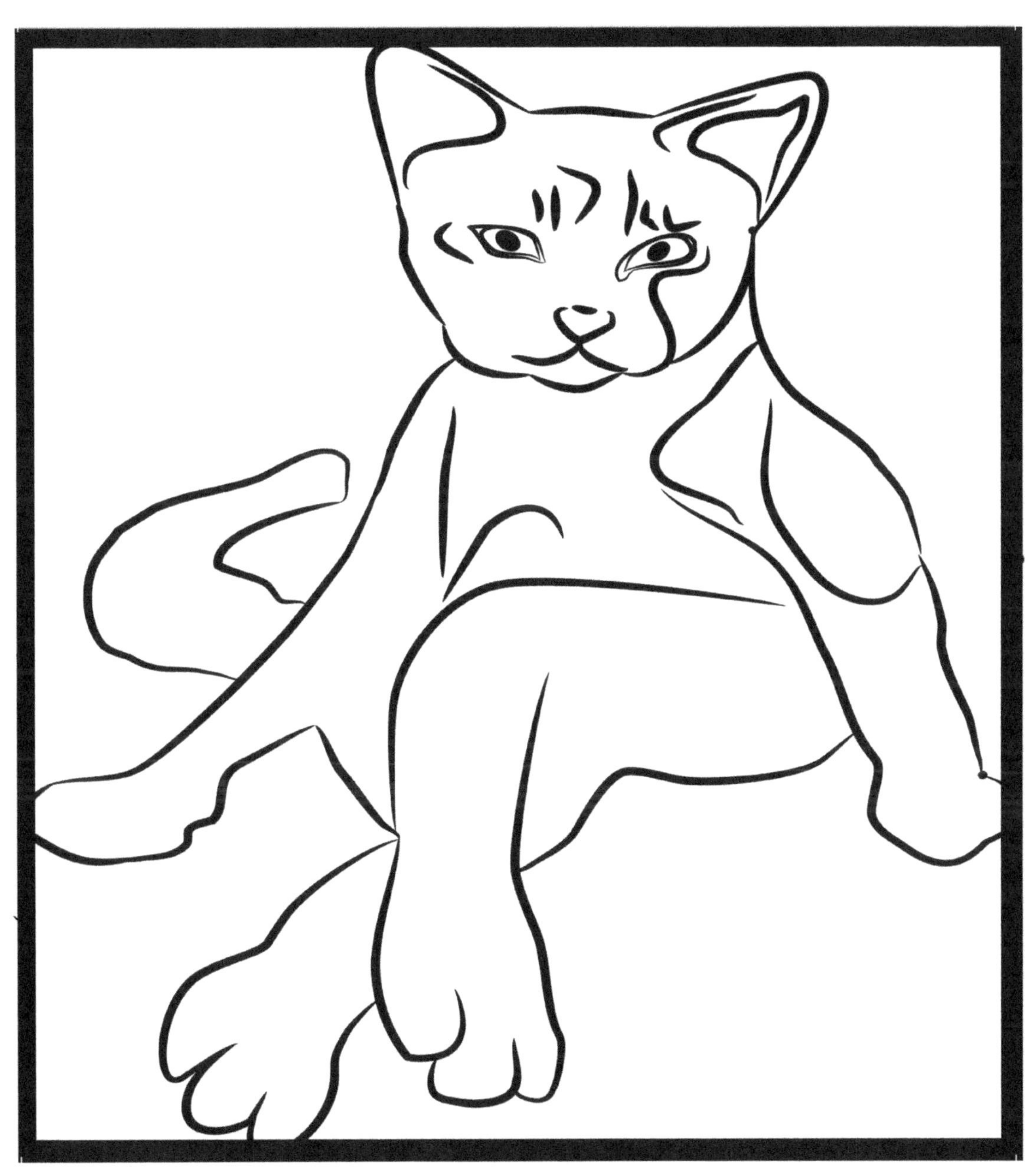

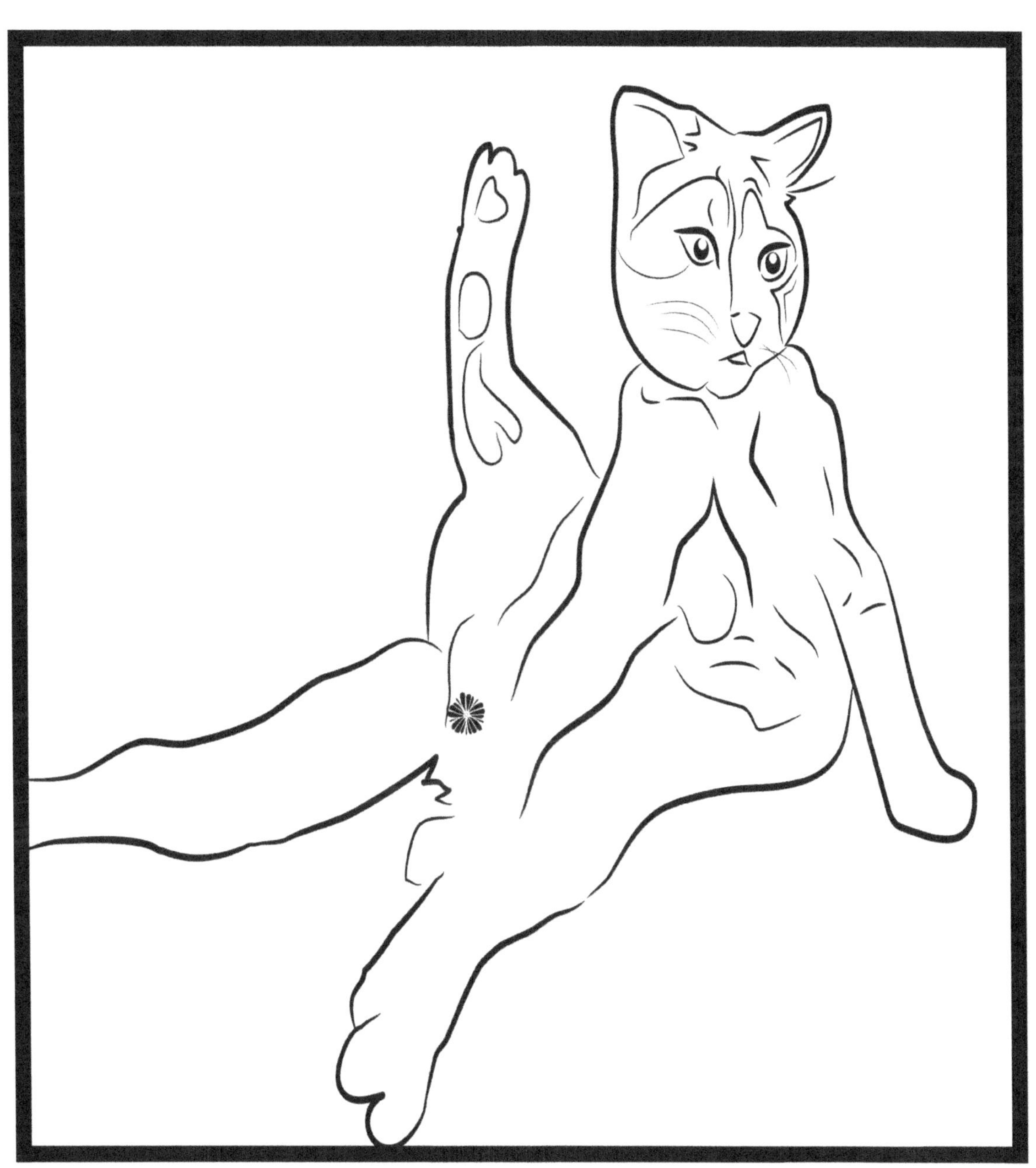

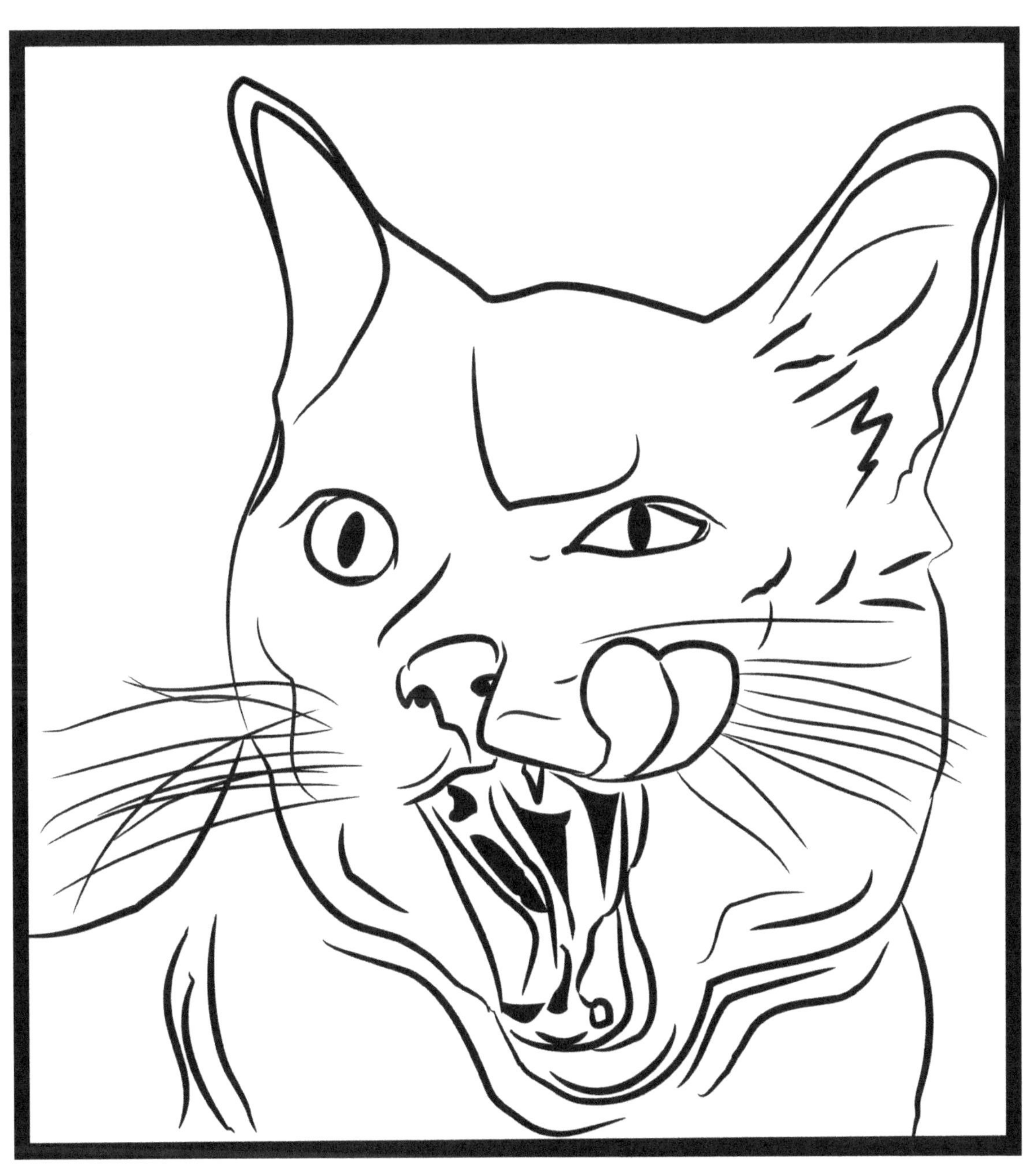

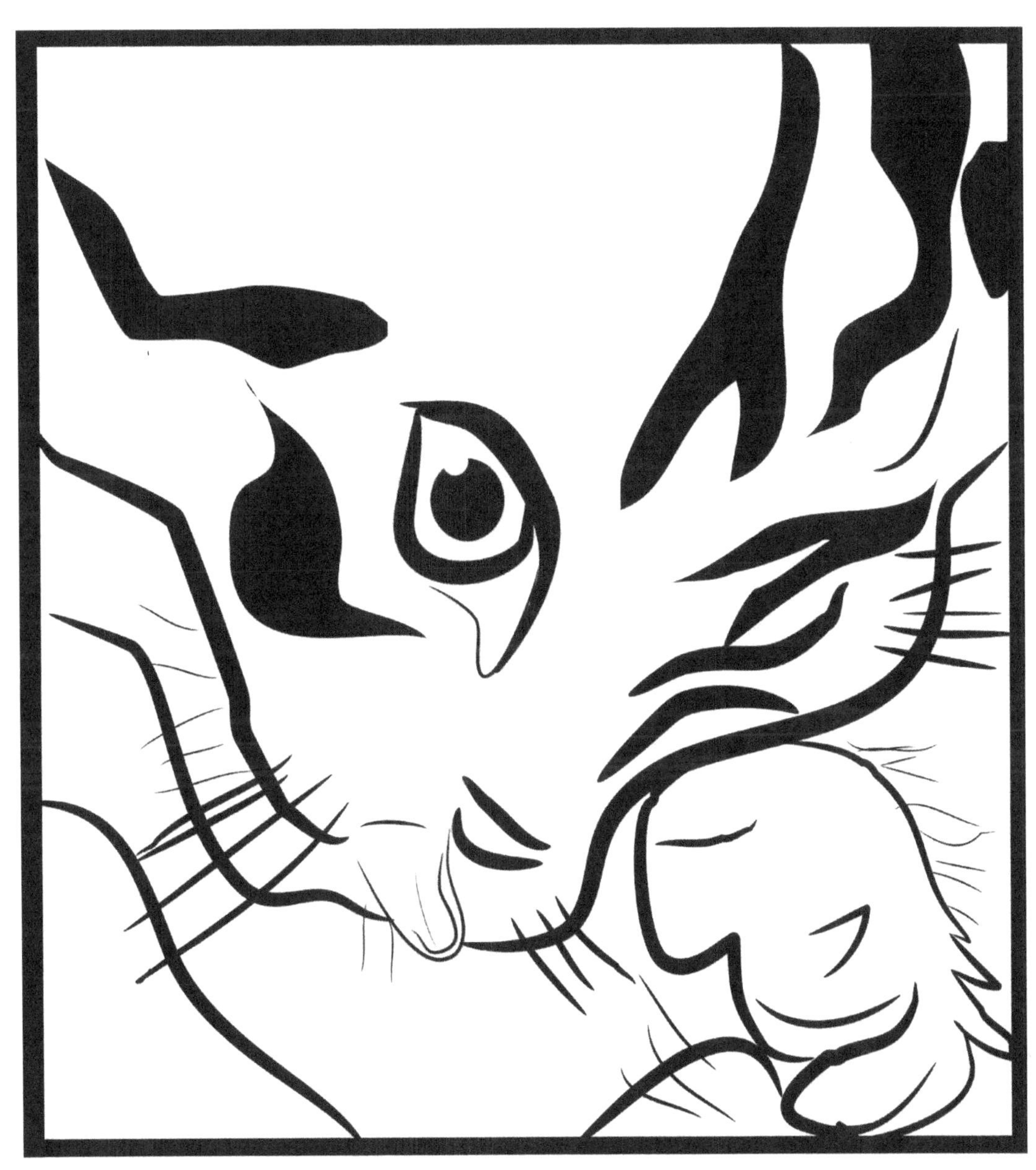

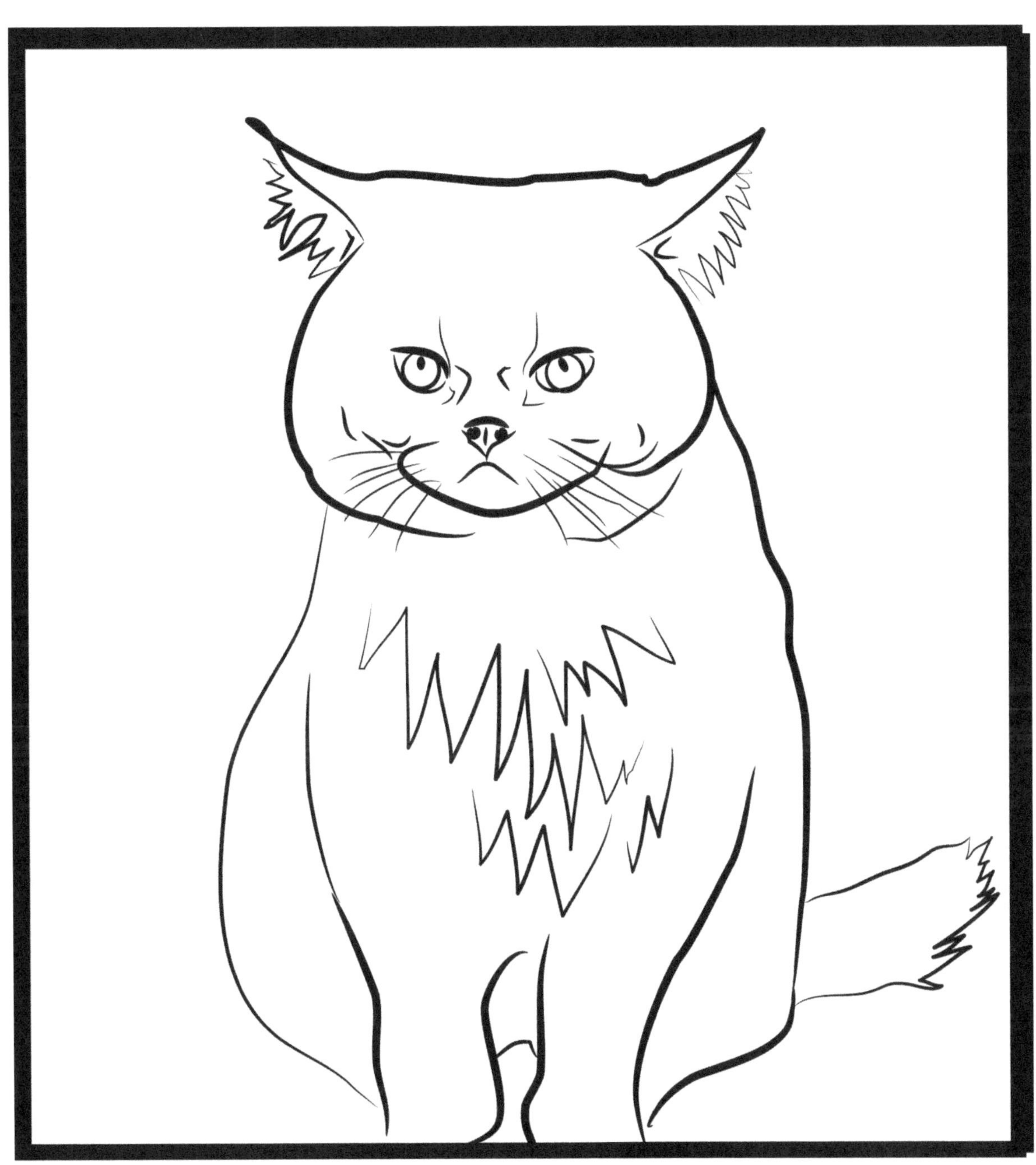

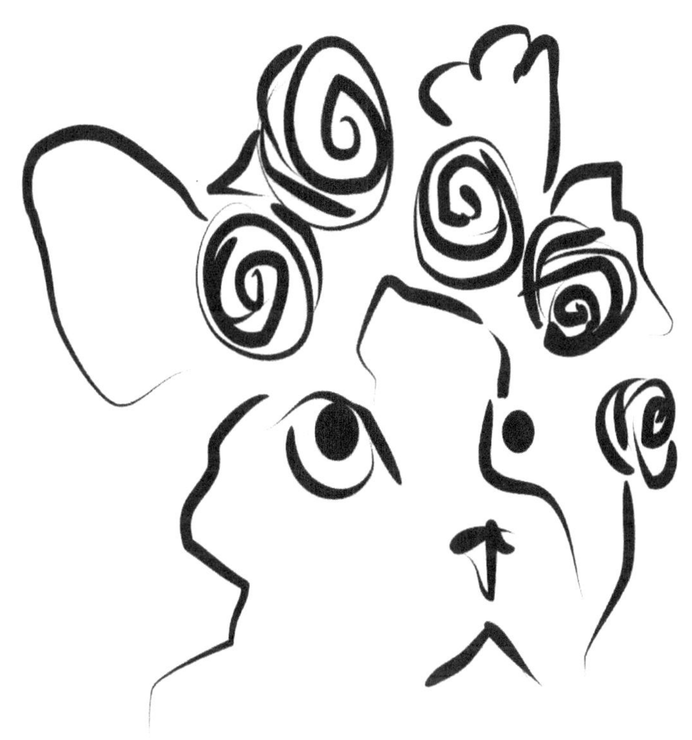